Just Another Boring Poetry Book

A collection of poems from 1997 to present day

Angela M Thomas

Agape First Publishing

First Edition

ISBN: 979-8-99303010-4

Library of Congress Control Number: [To be assigned]

Published by Agape First Publishing

PO Box 6202, Woodland Hills, CA 91365

Printed in the United States of America

Content Warning

This collection contains references to trauma, abuse, violence, and other sensitive topics. Reader discretion is advised.

For more information about the author, visit: social media: @autogirl83 (all platforms)

Contents

Reflection

I dedicate this book to all the ancestors who stand behind me rooting me on and to the four people who supported me that passed before I made it this far: Grandma, Charles, Grammy and Uncle. I miss and love you guys so much.

Acknowledgments

Hey, and thanks for buying, pirating, or renting my book. This is a collection of poems that I have written from the time I started writing way back in the seventh grade in Mrs. White's English class in 1997 at Bancroft Middle School to May 2025, when I graduated from CSUN (Cal State Northridge). Throughout the pages of this book, you will see how I have evolved as a poet and storyteller. If at any point you feel a move of the "Holy Spirit" (as the Baptist say) and want to show some appreciation, then drop me a line @autogirl83 across all social media platforms. I hope you enjoy my work. It was a labor of love.

I would love to pay acknowledgment to the wonderful literary journals that have accepted my work. One of them I worked on: *Kapu-Sans 2024 Volume 37, Northridge Review Fall 2025*: "Child Slave"; *Scarlet Review Vol. 2, Northridge Review Fall 2025*: "Bronze Limbs and Concrete Dreams"; *Northridge Review Fall 2025*: "Four Generations" and "Poem #5" (Which at the printing of this book has been changed to "Breaking").

I am deeply grateful for my time at California State University–Northridge. I'm especially thankful for the love and support of the faculty—Prof. Kimberly Young, Dr. Leilani Hall, Dr. Shubha Venuogopal, Prof. Martin Pousson, and Prof. Gina—each of whom are wonderful human beings that God placed in my life to help shape my voice. To my loving family, and especially to my husband, Keyon—my ride or die—who's had my back since 2008 and especially when I went back to school in 2019: I love you, dear. I also want to thank my two lovely editors Erin Kroncke and Sara Khayat without whom this book wouldn't be what it is today.

Blurbs

Ode to CSUN
CSUN a vibrant soul sucking for profit institution surrounded by beautiful
orange groves and methed out drug addicts.

Dreams

Hold fast to dreams
For if dreams die
Life is a broken-winged bird
That cannot fly.
Hold fast to dreams
For when dreams go
Life is a barren field
Frozen with snow.

Langston Hughes

Child

When I was a child, I talked like a child, I thought like a child, I reasoned like a child. First Corinthians 13:11a (NIV)

Agape First Publishing

My Family Lost

1997

Called him.
God called him to come home.
Took my uncle from us.
Stole him from us.
Dropped a rope down and said it's time to
go home Edward.
Let me take your hand and guide you.
Spoke the word to him and lead him to
freedom from drugs, gangs, and violence.
Gave him a life to live in the Lord's name
and prayer.
Drank the water from the fountain and
gave him a better life.

-In loving memory to Edward Renee Williams III a.k.a. Uncle

The Love I Have for You

01/09/1998

The love I have for you is deeper than the sea.

The love I have for you cannot be taken away from me.

The love I have for you is more than life itself.

The love I have for you can't be replaced by anyone else.

My Heart

01/1998

My heart is filled with so much pain.

And the pain just won't go away.

It hurts so deep inside.

That sometimes it makes me want to cry.

And it seems like nobody is there for me.

And sometimes I want to be alone.

My heart is filled with so much pain.

Why am I alone?

My Love

My love for you is deeper than the sea.

I would cross that sea for you just to get to you.

Why can't our love be for real?

Why can't it be the real deal?

My love for you is deeper than the sea,

Why can't it be the same for me?

Shining Star

As I sit here in my chair

I think about the good you have given me.

The love, the warmth and positivity.

Can't nothing take that away from me but hatred.

And that's something I don't have for you.

So, continue being the way you are cause you're like a shining star.

The Tree Sway

The trees sway in the wind like my love sways for you.

Like the wind it will always blow until God tells it to stop.

But nothing can stop us from loving each other.

I Need You Baby

08/25/1999

I need you baby to comfort me and hold
me.

I need you baby.

I need you now.

I need you to stop all this pain and hurt.

To keep the world from falling on top of
me

I need you to help me from falling off the
edge.

I need you baby; I need you now.

Love

Love is something not very many people have.

It comes from the heart and soul.

It's a feeling that can be held onto for a long period of time.

A person can only give out so much to one person.

If that love is toyed with

The person who gave it will be destroyed for the rest of their life.

So, don't play with my love.

The Beginning

01/2000

In our life we all are born. This is the first beginning of our life.

There is also a second beginning of life when we pass over to a new life.

This new life comes when you are saved and know the word of God and study it well.

The third beginning of life is the hereafter, when you are joined with your loved ones that passed before you.

So don't think of death as the end, think of it as a brand-new beginning.

-In loving memory of Dorothy Allen a.k.a. Grammy

Faith

08/2000

Faith is something that not many people believe in.

But me, I'm a strong believer in faith.

Without faith I can't live.

If you don't have faith, you don't have God.

And without God you're another lost soul caught up in society.

The fancy cars and money, that's not God

That's just material things.

So, keep faith in God and yourself or you're just another part of the problem.

Dying Black Generation

02/12/2001

I'm tired.

I'm sick and tired of brothers killin' brothers.

And why is this?

Is it because their parents tell them to?

Or their teachers tell them to.

No, it's because they're walking on the wrong territory.

Or they're wearing the wrong colors.

But I wonder.

Do they ever think who they killed?

It could be someone's brother, father, husband, uncle or even a boyfriend.

Do you ever think after killing a person?

Where you might end up

It's not at home with your homies.

It's in a cold jail cell spending 10 to 20 years.

All because you wanted to hang with the wrong crowd.

And do you ever think about that person's family?

They have now lost a loving member of their family.

Now all they have left is broken memories.

So, to all them gang bangers out there before you judge someone.

Look that person in the eye and think, "Am I ready to kill my own brother."

Laying Back

03/2001

Every night I lay in bed.
I think of only you
Thinking if you like me as much as I like
you.
Wishing you would tell me how you really
feel about me.
Things that girls only dream that their
guys would tell them.
So, don't hold back from me.
Because I'm someone you can count on.

True Love

04/09/2001

I look up and I see you standing in the hall,
you're laughing with your friends, and I
see you smile.
I want to come over and say, "Hi," but my
legs won't move.
I want to hold you in my arms, but my
arms won't lift.
I want to say how much I love your smile,
but my mouth won't speak.
The only thing I can do is look at you and
hope you look at me and at that moment
our eyes meet, we'll fall in love.
As our bodies move towards each other,
everything around us seems to disappear.
We're now in our own little world, where
only you and I exist.
As we get ready to speak, the bell rings.
We say our good-byes and go into class.
All the while both of us are hoping to see
each other the next day.

Child With the Perfect Smile

04/11/2001

Here standing before you is a child with
the perfect smile.
She laughs and jokes just like everyone else.
But deep down inside she cries.
She's crying for help, love, and attention.
She longs for the friendship others have
and the love that lovers give.
No one understands her, but God and
herself.
Try looking for a child with that perfect
smile before the world runs out of perfect
smiles.

Knowledge

11/2001

I hold in my hand the key to life.
I hold in my hand my mother's strife.

All the hard work it took to get me here.
To get there and then not go anywhere.

Not me, I'm going to college.
Because I have that knowledge.

I hold in my hand my future dreams.
I hold in my hand that master's degree.

To be a strong black woman in this day and
age.
It's always my generation flipping that
child's page.

I hold in my hand the power of knowledge.
I hold in my hand the tools for college.

This world is filled with so much hate right
now.
Everyone is always trying to bring us down.

And why is this?
We're always being dismissed.

Just because we're young.
The world labels us as dumb.

So, what I hold in my hand is my life

and I'm in command.

I hold in my hand my boyfriend's love.
I hold in my hand the whitest dove.

So pure and full of strife.
It's sad to see someone take their life.

That's how I feel sometimes.
It hurts so deep inside.

Woman

When I became a woman, I put the ways of childhood behind me. First Corinthians 13:11b (NIV)

Agape First Publishing

The Knife

See how long and sharp it is.

See how it shines in the light as you look at it, see how the handle feels in your hand.

Almost as if it's an extension of your arm.

You slash with it as it cuts through the air.

You admire how weightless it feels, how it almost feels like second nature to use it.

You slash through the air again, this time in a downward motion.

Blood sprays you in the face.

You want to stop but you can't.

You swing down again, more blood covers your face as you're stabbing it over and over again.

A sense of joy comes over you as you cut into the flesh, slicing at the muscles, the tendent, the fat.

A small voice rings in your ear, that starts to get louder.

They say, "So how do you like your meal?"

You look up from your plate and say I love
it, thank you for cooking tonight dear.

Weekend Warrior

08/2020

I was my grandmother's weekend warrior.

Almost every weekend for years as a child, we would go to the mall, either by bus or by car provided by a relative. We'd stroll around Stonewood or Del Amo Mall, shopping at Penny's (JCPenney) or Sears, looking for all the latest and greatest, mainly in clothes for me, to spend money on. She taught me how to sit at a table properly, how to wash my face and apply Vaseline in the morning and at night and she taught me how to pray. Then, after a while, I couldn't be her weekend warrior anymore. No longer a child, I was growing into a young woman. That's when she came into our lives.

God blessed her with a new weekend warrior, Amaya. And for 14 years, my grandmother became the mother figure that Amaya didn't have. Teaching her all the things that she felt Amaya would need. Like how to sit at a table properly and how to love the Lakers and the Dodgers. All the things she has taught me and when she knew she had nothing left to teach and Amaya was in excellent hands, God brought her home. I say all this to say this. Amaya, hold on to the teachings of grandma, though some of them might be old school. She taught you them for a reason. But knowing this, she knew you were in excellent hands, knowing your new mom would teach you things she could not. Grandma, I love you and I will forever walk around with your teachings.

-In loving memory of Melba J. Griffin a.k.a. Grandma

Are you lifting Him up?

05/2021

Do not take my name in vain
I remember that being one of the com-
mands of God

If I be lifted up, I will draw all men to Me
I think I remember Jesus saying that

I swear I heard a new commandment from
Jesus
Agape others the way I agape you, that is
how they will know you're one of mine?

I distinctly remember Jesus deciding cos-
mic destiny on if someone agaped
When you cared for the least of these you
cared for me?

Where is that reflection?
When do we model our namesake?

When we stop supporting the single
mother trying to feed her baby?
When we deport those looking to make a
better life for their families?
When we care more about the 1 percent's
wealth than the 99's destitute?

When do we show people who Jesus is
with our lives?
Not by rules, but by action?
Not by control, but by embrace?

Not by mammon, but by Christ?

When do we stop making Him into a Sun-
day only Father?
When do we make Him a way of life?
When do we agape like He did?
When do we lift Him up?

Break

The flower blooms in the sun and I know it's time to get up.

As I climb into my car, life waves hello to me in my missing rear-view mirror.

I scream curses to the sky as if someone will fall from it and fix *it*.

But no one does, no one ever does.

I continue to make lemonade out of the lemon's life keeps throwing at me.

But it comes out bitter/sweet.

I keep drinking it as if it's my life blood.

As if every drink is good to the last drop, when it's not.

I keep smiling until it hurts. I wear the mask until it breaks. Until I break.

I try to pick up the pieces but they dissolve in my hand.

I can't hide anymore; I can't hide the ugly truth anymore.

That I am a black woman.

A Black American living in a world that hates and does not love.

That exploits but does not care.

A world that I cannot escape.

Child Slave

Content Note: This poem contains references to child abuse, sexual violence, and trauma. Reader discretion is advised.

I was a child slave.
Raised to serve and do only what I was
told.
"Cook dinner," they say.
"Wash clothes," they say.
Do this, do that.
Every day for 15 years, I did what I was
told.

Did I ever get paid or rewarded for this?
Yes.
By being beat with extension cords and
paddles made of wood and leather belts.
Did my abusers ever care?
No, they laughed as they beat me.
Laughed at my pain, laughed at my tears,
they laughed at me.
So, what does a child slave do?
Grow up into an adult slave.
"Hey, girl, do this."
"Hey, bend over this way."
"Hey, give me a kiss."
They would say.
And I would do as I was told.

Because that's what love is, right?
A series of commands barked at you by
people saying they love you, right?
"Yo, girl, come here. Let me feel on you."
"Shut up! Who told you to speak?"

"Come here, you don't have a say. You do as I say."
They yell at me as they slap me. Hit me.
Rape me.
When do I have a say?
When does my voice become loud enough for them to hear it?
When do I take back what's mine?

Now.
The time to take back what is mine is now.
I wasn't made to be abused.
I wasn't made to be taken advantage of.
I was made to be loved.
Not through hate or abuse.
But through compassion, humility, and kindness
My body and mind were not made for you
It was made for me
Because only I know how to take care of me.

Preyed On

Did you pray for him mother?
Did you pray for the man that would be
my Captor for 9 months?
So that you could be my Savior?
Did you pray for him like you preyed on
me not to leave?
Did the prayer dribble from your lips like
blood?
Did it fall from your mouth like teeth?
Did you speak the words as if they were
your last breath?
Did you mother?

How many times did you fast until he
showed up?
How many times did you speak in tongues
in your prayer closet making sure I would
never want to leave?
Did you pray for the pregnancy that would
almost kill me when I had to make the
tough decision to terminate it?

Did you pray for him to abuse me?
break me?
traumatize me?
for you to save me?

Did you pray for him to shatter my self-es-
teem?
Make me feel less than?
Tried to pull me away from my family, iso-

late me?
So, when I returned you could be sure that
I would never leave again, cause leaving
would trigger me?

But you did all that didn't you?
I will never forget the smirk on your face
when I came to you, as if you prophesied
all this would happen.
That you and your so-called "god" orches-
trated this for me.

Why did you hate me so?
What did I do to draw your contempt?
Or did you just need something in your life
that you thought you could control?
When will you ever repent?

Was I always your prey?
Was I always your puppet?
Did you draw meaning for your life
through my suffering?
Why did you even have me?
That is right for a slave that could bring
you sanity.
Thank the Lord for a true God that saved
me.

Four Generations Removed

I am four generations removed from slav-
ery
Four generations from my ancestors want-
ing the best for me

Four generations of a lineage they tried to
erase.
A group of people they tried to replace

My mother is three generations removed
She did not take advantage of the educa-
tion opportune presented to her
She let them slip through her fingers.

Grandma too.

Great-grandmother was one generation
removed
One generation from being beaten to her
tomb.

One generation from a beating she would
catch
But not enough removed to forget the
smell of burning flesh.

The Rich Burn and The poor drown

The Rich sit on top of their hills looking
down.
Wondering why they chose to be down
there
Does it mean they deserve to lose every-
thing?

The Rich Burn and the poor drown

The poor look up at the Rich and wish
they can be up there with them.
Not knowing what it took to get there.
As they drown in debt to live above their
means

The Rich Burn and the poor drown

The Rich live in places that the poor can't
reach until it rains.
The Rich have things that the poor want
to obtain until it goes up in flames.

The Rich Burn and the poor drown

When the levees broke who was supposed
to maintain
To keep the poor from drowning
When a city burns down who is to blame.
To keep the Rich from frowning.
Can we come together long enough to

keep the poor from drowning and the
Rich from burning?

American Sonnet for the Box They Call Reform

Can I tell you about the place where hu-
mans sleep with other humans in steel
boxes? Not metaphor—actual bars. The
watchers call it housing. They play a game:
let them out to lift iron until muscles
scream, to toss a striped sphere through a
ring like glory hinges on orange arcs. When
two wrestle, the loser blooms red—straw-
berry jam, let's say—until yield is forced.
The winner isn't praised. Only the jam
gets wiped away. A nurse restores silence
to the skin. Later, a tray offers balance:
protein, carbs, a lesson in portions. Be
good, get more. Be bad, stay hungry. When
enough days rot off the bone, they're re-
leased—unzipped back into the wilderness
called freedom.

Bronze Limbs and Concrete Dreams

A Poem in the Voice of Josephine Baker

I was born where the pavement sweats,
where the sun drapes its gold on the backs
of brown girls
who learn to dance before they learn to
dream.
Where the sirens wail like lost souls at mid-
night,
and the streetlights hum secrets only the
stray dogs know.

Mama worked her fingers into threads of
prayer,
stitched rent money into the seams of sec-
ondhand dresses.
She taught me how to smile with my whole
body,
to move like joy had no cage,
like the world was an open stage waiting
for my feet to claim it.

South Central taught me rhythm before
love,
how to sway between cracked sidewalks
and stolen glances,
how to spin away from hungry hands and
whispering corners,
how to laugh in the face of a city that didn't
always love me back.

The boys on the block called me trouble,
said my hips spoke a language they weren't

old enough to understand.
I told them I was made of music,
of jazz notes and Sunday morning hallelu-
jahs,
of the stories my grandmother carried
from the Delta
and the freedom I knew was waiting some-
where past Crenshaw.

I dreamed in sequins, in feathers, in soft-lit
stages
where the only bullets were the ones shot
from cameras,
where the applause was louder than the
police knocks.
Where my body belonged to movement,
not survival.

So, I danced.
On the pavement, on the bus stop bench-
es, in the aisles of the corner store.
I danced until the city couldn't hold me
anymore.
Until my name was more than a whisper.

And when I left—
when I flew over the cracked streets and
neon liquor signs,
over the boys who swore they'd marry me
someday,
over the prayers Mama stitched into my
coat—
I carried South Central in the arch of my
back,
in the tilt of my chin,
in the way I made the world watch me
without ever asking for permission.

Concrete Garden

We don't call it wild
but it grows—
dandelions splitting sidewalk seams
like they've got secrets to tell
from underneath the city's skin.

Graffiti vines curl up brick walls,
colors blooming like defiance
in aerosol and sweat.
A rusted fence becomes a trellis
for trash bags that catch the wind
like prayer flags in mourning.

There is nature here.
In the busted hydrant
singing summer into the street,
in pigeons that know
how to outlive
the rat, the hawk, the cop,
the noise.

We don't hike here,
we navigate—
broken glass like dewdrops,
bodega neon glowing
against dusk like fireflies.

Mama plants basil in an old paint can,
says it'll keep the mosquitoes down
and the ancestors close.
She blesses it with tap water

and the soft hum
of a Lauryn Hill track.

This garden don't ask for praise.
It knows what it is—
gritty, cracked,
alive anyway.

Underpainting

Inspired by Terrance Hayes' "Bob Ross Paints Your Portrait"

Close your eyes, I am going to paint you a
picture.
Do you see her?
The beautiful black woman there painted
on the canvas.
Painted in shades of brown and bronze.
Golds and reds.

Do you see her hair?
How it starts off black, then transitions to
purple curly
locks that cascade down her back and
around her face.

We see that at the front of her mind is her
family.
As we move further in, we find the hurt
and the pain of the past.
The part of her memory she would like to
forget but can't.

As we dig a little deeper, we find past lovers
and friends.
A family that is gone but not forgotten.
At the back of her mind is the one who
created her.
The one who has been in control of her life
the whole time.
The one who created the moon and the
stars.
And her voice. Period

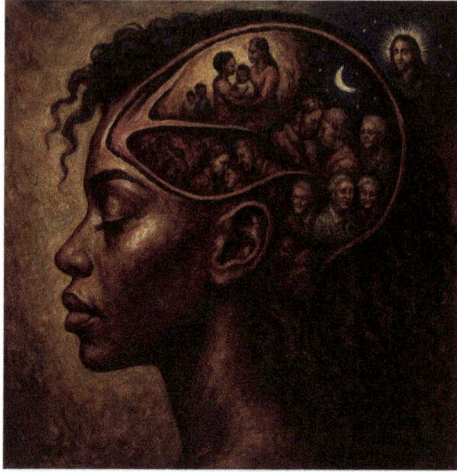

A Poem for Moms

Hey Mom, I see you over there—
rockin' that French fry in your hair.
Kids running wild, chaos in the air,
just trying to survive without falling down
the stairs.

Let me tell you, it *will* get better.
It's going to be okay.
So what if you forgot deodorant today?
Honestly—can't even smell you anyway.

Wearing the same bra three days straight?
And those panties from... what, day two or
eight?
It's fine.

Left that diaper on an hour too long?
Passed out mid-sex like a bedtime song?
Girl. It's okay.

You've got another day to get it "right,"
another day to fight the good fight,
another chance to be beautifully imper-
fect—
and that is perfectly okay.

His Love

He holds me close in his arms.
The smell of morning on his breath.

Through his glasses I see his milk chocolate
brown eyes
and they give me wonderful butterflies

I melt into him and he holds me safe in his
embrace
and I love how he makes my heart race.

The Fire Keeps Blooming

They said nothing grows here—
this cracked-up slab of city, where prayers
bounce off brick and fall into sirens.

But look—
there's a woman rising from the sidewalk,
hips like prophecy, mouth full of God.
Her feet, dusted with the ashes of her fore-
mothers,
know how to dance around landmines.

She carries children in one arm,
history in the other—
stained hands still soft enough
to braid love into pain.

She sings in a voice stitched from
James Baldwin's sighs and Grandma's
humming.
A melody of "not today," and "try me,"
and "hallelujah anyway."

She walks past the levees they forgot to fix.
Past the burning towers and flooded base-
ments.
And when they ask her how she survived—

She just smiles, opens her palm,
and says: "The fire keeps blooming."

TRUE LOVE (Part II: The Days After)

The next day comes,
and I search for you in every corner of the
crowd—
between slamming lockers
and the shuffle of feet on linoleum floors.

There—
a flash of your jacket,
the sound of your laugh echoing off the
walls.
My heart stirs,
hope rising like morning light.

This time,
I don't freeze.
My steps are unsure,
but they move.
Closer.
Closer.

We lock eyes again—
a flicker,
a silent question:
Do you remember yesterday, too?

And then you smile.
Not just a casual grin,
but one that lingers,
like you were waiting for me,
too afraid to say so.

You say, "Hey."
Just that.
And somehow, it's everything.

We talk—
not much,
but enough to feel the world shift again.
Names,
favorites,
music,
movies—
just the beginning of something
soft and unspoken.

Chood

Bright smile
Infectious laugh
Smarter than people gave you credit for.
You were the little big brother I didn't
want but needed
And I realized it too late, now you're on the
other side of heaven's door.

No more late-night jokes
No more silly antics
No more kept secrets from parents.

Remember that time you cracked you
head on the table
As we all dance to "Hammer Man" a 90's
staple
And when you pulled the fire alarm at the
hospital
You were only embarrassed a little

Remember when Donneé came home and
he and Mark started to "toughen" you up.
I cried for them to leave you alone because
I wanted to protect you.
For you to start throwing blows back, no
longer a pup.
I was so proud of you.

And how fly you use to dress
Always wearing your Sunday's best.

I miss you most of all little bro
But I know you up there helping Jesus get
ready for His return.
And Jesus is going to look fly if you helping
Him, you know.

-In loving memory of Charles L. Hood III a.k.a. Chood

Reflection

For now we see only a reflection as in a mirror;
then we shall see face to face. Now I know in part;
then I shall know fully, even as I am fully known. First
Corinthians 13:12 (NIV)

Agape First Publishing

My Family Loss

God called him.
Summoned him home,
lifted my uncle from our grasp—
a sudden theft wrapped in grace.

He dropped a rope from heaven,
whispered, *Edward, it's time.*
Took his hand with a gentleness
none of us could match.

Spoke salvation into his bones,
led him from the shadows—
drugs, gangs, violence—
into a light we could only pray for.

The Lord gave him new breath,
a name washed in prayer.
He drank from the fountain
and rose,
finally whole.

The Love I have For You

The love I hold for you runs deeper than
the sea—
a current that no storm can steal from me.
It's more than breath, more than bone and
skin;
a fire that burns quietly, steady within.

No force can shake it loose or draw it thin,
no other soul could take the place you're
in.
It is not fleeting, nor made for show—
this love is the root from which I grow.

My Heart

My heart carries a weight
that words can't lift.
A sorrow so rooted,
it hums beneath my ribs,
aching without end.

The hurt runs deep—
deeper than tears can reach—
and some days,
the silence around me feels
like the only thing that understands.

I search for comfort,
but the room stays empty.
I pull away,
not because I want to,
but because solitude feels safer
than the echo of absence.

My heart is heavy with pain.
And still I wonder—
why must I carry it alone?

My Love

My love for you runs deeper than the sea—
endless, uncharted, and wild.
I would brave every wave,
cross every storm-swept mile,
just to reach you.

But why does this love feel like a dream
I'm the only one believing?
Why can't it be real—
solid as stone,
true as tide?

My love runs deep,
so why does yours stay
shallow at the shoreside?

Shining Star

As I sit here in quiet reflection,
I hold close the good you've given me—
the love, the warmth,
the steady light of your presence.

Nothing can steal that from me—
not time, not distance,
not even bitterness,
because I carry no hatred for you.

So, keep being who you are,
unchanged and true—
a constant in my sky,
shining like the star you've always been.

The Trees Sway

The trees sway in the wind,
gentle and sure—
just like my love moves for you,
constant, unwavering.

Like the wind,
it stirs through seasons,
never ceasing
until God Himself commands it still.

But even then,
not heaven or earth
could silence this love
we carry for each other.

I Need You, Baby

I need you, baby—
to hold me close,
to be the calm in my storm.

I need you now.
Right now.

To quiet the ache
and soften the hurt
before the weight of the world
comes crashing down.

I need your arms
like a ledge needs steady ground—
to catch me
before I fall too far.

I need you, baby.
I need you now.

Love

Not everyone holds it,
not everyone honors it.

It rises from the heart,
from the soul's quiet chambers,
and when it's real,
it stays.

But love is not endless.
One heart can only pour so much
into another
before it runs dry.

And if that love is misused,
if it's turned into a game—
the giver doesn't just walk away.
They carry the ruin.
They live with the pain.

So, hear me when I say:
Don't play with my love.
It's the truest part of me.

The Beginning

In this life, we are all born—
our first beginning.
The breath, the cry,
the light of this world greeting us
for the very first time.

But there is a second beginning,
a sacred one—
when the soul awakens,
and we come to know God.
To walk in His word,
to be saved by His grace—
this, too, is life renewed.

And then, there is the third—
the final beginning,
when we pass from this world
into the arms of the next.
A homecoming.
A reunion with those we've loved and lost.

So do not fear death.
It is not the end.
It is a doorway to forever,
the beginning of beginnings.

Faith

Faith—
not everyone believes in it.
But I do.
I believe with my whole being.

Without faith,
I couldn't make it through the day.
Because faith is more than hope—
it's the lifeline to God.

And without God,
you're just another soul
adrift in a world
that praises the wrong things—
fast cars, quick money,
shiny lies.

That's not God.
That's distraction.
That's emptiness dressed up in gold.

So, keep your faith.
In Him.
In yourself.

Because without it,
you're not just lost—
you're part of what's breaking this world.

Dying Black Generation

I'm tired.
Tired of brothers killin' brothers—
of blood spilled over blocks,
of lives lost to colors,
of futures shattered for pride.

And why?
Is it because their parents told them to?
Their teachers?
No.
It's because they crossed a street
they weren't "supposed" to cross,
wore a color
they weren't "supposed" to wear.

But do they ever stop—
even for a second—
and wonder who they've taken?

It could be someone's son.
Someone's brother,
father, husband,
uncle, boyfriend—
someone loved.
Someone needed.

And after the shot rings out,
what's left?

Not a badge of honor.
Not a celebration.

Just cold steel and concrete—
a jail cell
where time moves slow and regret moves
fast.
All because you wanted to prove
you were down with the wrong crew.

Do you ever think about the ones left be-
hind?
The mothers who won't sleep.
The sisters who won't stop crying.
The children who won't understand
why Daddy's not coming home.

All they have now
are broken memories
and a pain that never leaves.

So, to all the gang bangers out there—
before you pull the trigger,
before you pass judgment,
look your brother in the eye and ask your-
self:

**"Am I really ready to kill my own
brother?"**

Laying Back

Each night, I lie awake,
thinking only of you—
wondering if your thoughts
drift to me,
the way mine float to you.

Do you feel what I feel?
Or am I holding all of this alone?

I wish you'd say it—
those words girls dream of hearing,
the kind that turn silence into something
sacred.

Don't hold back.
Not with me.

I'm not just hoping for love—
I'm here,
steady,
someone you can count on.

True Love

I see you—
standing in the hall,
laughing with your friends,
and that smile...
that smile stops the world.

I want to walk over,
say *hi,*
but my legs forget how to move.
I want to hold you close,
but my arms stay frozen at my sides.
I want to tell you
how much I love your smile,
but my voice—
it hides behind my heart.

So, I just watch,
hoping,
praying,
that maybe you'll look my way.

And when our eyes meet—
just for a moment—
it feels like falling.
Like flying.

The noise fades.
The hallway disappears.
And it's just us,
suspended in time—
a world where nothing else matters.

But then the bell rings.
And reality returns.
We part with soft goodbyes,
each of us carrying the same hope—

tomorrow,
maybe tomorrow,
we'll get another chance.

Child With The Perfect Smile

She stands before you—
a child with the perfect smile.
Bright.
Unshaken.
The kind of smile that lights a room
before she ever speaks.

She laughs,
she plays,
she masks the ache with ease.

But beneath that perfect smile
are tears she never shows—
a quiet weeping,
a longing that won't let go.

She cries for love,
for someone to see her,
really see her—
not the smile,
but the girl behind it.

She yearns for friendship,
for arms that hold without judgment,
for the kind of love
that doesn't ask her to pretend.

No one understands—
no one,
except God
and the fragile strength she hides within.

So, look closely.
Look with more than your eyes.

Find the child
with the perfect smile
before the world
steals all the perfect smiles away.

Knowledge

I hold in my hand the key to life.
I carry my mother's struggle,
her sacrifice, her strife—
every late night, every prayer,
poured into getting me here.

To arrive,
only to stop short?
Not me.

I'm going to college.
Because I carry something sacred:
knowledge.

I hold in my hand
the shape of future dreams,
the weight of a master's degree
etched with hope and endurance.

To be a strong Black woman
in this day and age—
it means breaking cycles,
it means turning the page
for every child watching,
waiting.

I hold in my hand
the power to rise,
the tools to build,
to claim what's mine.

This world—
it's heavy with hate,
ready to crush
every dream we create.

And why?
Because we're young.
Because we dare.
They label us *foolish*,
like we don't care.

But I know better.
I hold in my hand
my life—
and I'm in command.

I hold in my hand
my boyfriend's love,
and the quiet hope
of a snow-white dove—

so pure,
so fragile in its flight,
and yet,
so easy to destroy.

That's how I feel sometimes.
Like something innocent,
dying slow beneath the weight.

The pain runs deep.
But I still rise.

Because I hold in my hand
not just sorrow,
but strength.
Not just dreams,
but destiny.